# THE VOCAL LIBRARY

WITH 2 CDs OF FULL PERFORMANCES AND ACCOMPANIMENTS

# Folksongs in Recital

## Low Voice

### 14 Concert Arrangements by Richard Walters

T0081534

Cover painting: Jasper F. Cropsey, *Bareford Mountains,* 1850, oil on canvas, 58.6 x 101.8 cm, Brooklyn Museum, New York

ISBN-13: 978-1-4234-2135-1
ISBN-10: 1-4234-2135-3

## HAL•LEONARD®
### CORPORATION

7777 W. BLUEMOUND RD. P.O. BOX 13819 MILWAUKEE, WI 53213

Visit Hal Leonard Online at
**www.halleonard.com**

# Contents

Singers on the CD:
*Kathleen Sonnentag, mezzo-soprano; **Kurt Ollmann, baritone

Pianist on the CD:
Richard Walters

# Arranger's Preface

Folksongs are an expression of humanity. In an era before commercial music and recording, folksongs survived by being handed down from one singer to another.

All of the songs in this collection are American in origin but one. The exception is "I Know Where I'm Goin'," included because of a concept I had for the *Johnny Songs* set. The songs date from the 18th century to c.1900. Many of these concert settings were originally published in the 2002 Vocal Library release *American Folksongs*.

The book/CD package of *Folksongs in Recital* allows one to hear a recording of the material with the arranger/composer as pianist, as well accompaniments recorded for practice. The recordings are not necessarily to be imitated, but should be interesting to any potential performer of this music. I am very interested in phrasing as a composer, but hesitate to notate every detail of how each phrase is to be shaped, so as to allow artists some freedom in performance. However, the recordings may help a singer and pianist understand more thoroughly my compositional intentions.

"Arrangement" can mean many things, depending on the context. These concert arrangements are in the spirit of art songs for voice and piano. Even though they are based on existing melodies, these settings were approached as I would any fully conceived composition, attempting to create an organic wholeness and overarching design for each. I chose songs that speak to the composer in me, with various sources, many times with more than one source for a tune and words. I very occasionally altered a word for modern comprehension.

These concert arrangements were conceived for classical singers and pianists in recital situations. The writing is for the same classical voice a singer would use in any art song literature. Despite being folksongs, a simpler "folk" vocal sound is not appropriate for these particular arrangements. However, a singer may experiment with diction, creating a vernacular spirit in dialect as appropriate. Some singers would not be comfortable with a southern accent, but that may be fitting for some selections; it is not necessary, however. Remember that however poetic the sentiments, these are words of ordinary folk, not educated classes. Approach the diction in them in the same way that you would an opera character of that ilk.

It will probably become apparent that these folksong settings have a dramatic temperament. Give me a little tune, an implied character, and I tend to turn it into a mini-drama every time without necessarily having that intent. I would advise singers and pianists performing these arrangements to find the drama built into the music and the character in the song, treading into an operatic spirit at times. The settings work best for developed voices that can create a substantial climax. In general, they are intended for mature collegiate singers or those beyond that level.

I suppose that I have an Americana streak in me that comes out in this material. Actually, I detest the sound of a composer assuming an Americana style in an artificial way. I can only guess that my early childhood in the rural South combined with my coming of age in the Midwest somehow has given me a natural affinity with American folksong. You can judge for yourself if that is true.

I am more than pleased if you would like to perform my concert arrangements. (If you record them for commercial release, you must seek a mechanical license, as you would for recording any copyrighted material.) I would like to gently point out that these concert arrangements are copyrighted works. I have occasionally been deflated by singers and pianists who have felt that the word "arrangement" on my many published such works is a signal to fiddle with the note content in whatever way they like.

To date I have published about 60 concert settings for voice and piano. This began in the summer of 1991. By then I had been in the field of music publishing seven years, and had already realized that unless I was out there developing a public composing career (difficult to do with a more than full-time life in music publishing), I could not justify publishing my own original compositions. Yet I continued to write music, and continue to do so today. I had an idea of fully composed arrangements instead, because I could imagine that treatments of appealing songs might be useful and intriguing to singers. Such work could be marketed in a way that my original art songs could not be marketed. During July of 1991 the musical concept of "concert arrangement" for classical singer and pianist quickly emerged as I composed ten settings of songs by Rodgers, Porter and Gershwin (published in *Popular Ballads for Classical Singers*), and two carol settings (first published in *The Classical Singer's Christmas Album*) in the space of two weeks. After that first burst there was more to explore in the genre over many years, especially inspired by regular work with tenor Steven Stolen and mezzo-soprano Kathleen Sonnentag.

## COMMENTS ON THE SONGS

### Beware, Oh, Take Care

This song could be sung by either a woman or a man. A woman's exaggerated outrage can create comedy, a parody on female helplessness in determining her own desires. I can imagine that there are women who could sing about the "dangerous" attractions of these young men, and though singing "Beware," the subtext would really be a flirtatious, "come hither." A man who is a good actor could create a different twist with a more tart and sexy sarcasm, or approach it as a sermon-like warning played broadly for comic effect.

### Bill Groggin's Goat

In this good-natured corny joke of a song it may help the pianist to realize that I thought of the brief piano interludes as the goat chomping on something crunchy. A performance should set up the last line of the song in the same way that one would set up the punch line of a joke.

### How Can I Keep from Singing

This tune was published in Robert Lowry's *Bright Jewels for the Sunday School* (1869), though his implied claim of authorship is doubtful; the tune and words are more likely of folk origin. The text has sometimes been attributed to Anna Warner (author of the first verse of "Jesus Loves Me"), but that credit is also unproven. "Singing" in the text could be a metaphor for speaking out in the face of injustice, as well as the more direct meaning of enjoying the pure pleasure of singing. I originally composed this concert setting as a duet more than a decade ago (published in the Vocal Library collection *American Folksongs*), and later adapted this solo version.

### I Gave My Love a Cherry

This tender Kentucky love song is sometimes called "The Riddle Song." "A chicken when it's pippin'" in the last verse refers to the undeveloped bird in the egg (*pippin'* is a dialect version of *peeping*). It may feel natural to slow down a bit for the third verse, although I did not want to dictate that with a firm marking. At the phrase "the story that I love you, it has no end," I invite the singer to come up with something particularly and individually expressive. If you cannot sing the optional high notes at the end softly and sweetly, then take the lower option.

### Nine Hundred Miles

This blues folksong probably dates from the late 19th century or first decade of the 20th century. The character singing the song is a railroad worker. The singer should be aware of the melodic blue note in a phrase such as "I'll be home tomorrow night" (at the top of the second page, for instance). I hope that I don't have to point out that the design of the arrangement is a steam engine train, starting with spurts, then a slow roll, gradually building up to full speed. The train passes out of sight at the end. The final note, on the word "blow," need not be held as long as is notated. This same tune is also associated with the words of the African-American spiritual "Gospel Plow."

**Once I Had a Sweetheart**

Women's folksongs are often about waiting for someone, or songs of heartbreak, which may reflect an apparently subservient role to men's lives in the culture of times past. "Once I Had a Sweetheart" is an example, the folksong equivalent of a torch song. She rocks herself in her sadness, obsessing over her lover's departure and her aloneness. Her emotions become more fully expressed as the setting moves forward, reaching operatic abandon on the final page.

**Sail Around**

This song is usually called "The Old Cow Died." I changed the title to "Sail Around" in my setting, because I had a hard time imagining the introduction: "I will sing 'The Old Cow Died.'" That sounds like something comic is about to follow. This song is anything but comedy. Cattle were the livelihood of a ranch of the American plains; the death of a susceptible old cow from cholera was an indicator of a probable coming epidemic and possible financial ruin. This is a mournful dialogue song between a son or daughter, or a cowhand, and the matron of the ranch. Worry becomes apparent in the obsessive repetition of the refrain. Feel free to expand the phrase at the top of the last page. The image in my mind on the repeated "sail around" phrase at the end of the setting was of the buzzards circling low to the ground.

**Shenandoah**

"Shenandoah" is traditionally called a chanty, but probably of the river variety rather than of the sea. It is possibly from the early decades of the 19th century. Two verses first appeared in print in a *Harpers* magazine article in 1882. Shenandoah was an Indian chief; the character in the song fell in love with Shenandoah's daughter on a westward bound journey. The regret of leaving behind a love and a beloved place is also stated. The emotions are of a man going away, probably never to return, heading out to the mythical, unknown West. I conceived the operatic climax of the setting as on a vessel, rocking and moving forward against the current. It is the emotional juncture of the pain of leaving with the overwhelming expanse and pull of the vast West, and all the adventure, promise and danger held there. This famous song, an icon of Americana, has a mysterious power, and conjures strong emotions in me that I cannot explain.

**Single Girl**

The woman in the song seems a bit like a comedian, making light of the hardships of her married life. The performance needs a sense of fun and insouciance. After the interlude at the top of the last page, as if with a big sigh of relief, the hectic pace of her domestic life slows down, as does the music, as she tells of putting the children to bed. The mood suddenly shifts to darkness when we learn that she wanted to get them out of sight before the return of her drunken husband. We can guess that in this miserable marriage he probably strikes and abuses her.

**The Streets of Laredo**

Also known as the "Cowboy's Lament," this American song is based on the Irish songs "A Handful of Laurel" and "The Bard of Armagh." Though the date of origin is unknown (probably 19th century), the lyrics of "The Streets of Laredo" were first published in 1927 in *The American Songbag*, edited by the poet Carl Sandburg. There are many verses, and I chose to omit some in my setting. There are various versions of this famous ballad, which has been recorded many times by various artists. The dying young cowboy, who undoubtedly has led a rough and lonely life, becomes sentimental as death approaches, revealing a surprisingly poetic character. This arrangement is conceived dramatically, with remorse leading into the piano interlude. At the climax of emotion in the interlude, his pain and failing breath motivate the sudden switch to soft music at the top of the penultimate page. That fairly long stretch allows the singer/actor to move from the agony of remorse to the "sleepiness" of inevitable death settling in. By the last verse he is in an altered state, with deluded visions as the life leaves his body. The performer's challenge is to communicate this dying energy in a way that retains clear diction and allows the voice to still carry and resonate. It is the equivalent of a stage death in opera. I recommend that the singer closes his eyes by the final line, as the cowboy gently dies.

I wrote this arrangement in my head on a long bicycle ride of several hours along the shore of Lake Michigan. I worked through the material as an actor would (a common compositional habit for me), looking for the character and subtext, deciding whether to contain the sentiment of the song with a restrained approach, or instead, to try to go past sentiment into something more organically dramatic to allow the character to emerge. I chose the latter approach. After trying to imagine who this young man was, and considering how I would portray him and his song in a setting, I found myself sobbing for him and his fate as I rode along. I only hope I got some of that emotion on the page. I wonder if it would be revealing too much to state that the musical inspiration for the final verse of the arrangement came from Benjamin Britten's death aria for Billy Budd.

## *Johnny Songs*

This set is conceived to be sung by one character, whose love for Johnny is portrayed through the progression of four songs, from youthful infatuation to anxiously awaiting his return from war.

### I Know Where I'm Goin'

The woman in the song is conflicted between her wishes for her future as a respectable woman, with all the comforts of affluence, and her love for the handsome but penniless Johnny. Though this young woman says she knows where she is going, my setting implies that she does not in the first verse, with a piano part of static and vague direction. She temporarily (and somewhat artificially) brightens up as she describes her fantasy of a fine and rich life, but just as quickly settles down into a dreamy surrender to the reality of her love for Johnny. The brief interludes (marked "slowly"), allow for some transition between these various emotions of the verses. Her emotions swell to grand expression in the last verse, defiant and swooning.

### The Cruel War Is Raging

Her determination to remain with Johnny, even though he has been called to the army, becomes more and more insistent, to the desperate and farfetched idea of disguising herself as a man. She makes one last operatic appeal to him to get his "yes," at the end. I think that it is possible that Johnny just says "yes" temporarily to end her pleas and quiet her.

### Johnny Has Gone for a Soldier

The "yes" at the end of the previous song was a false promise, leaving her alone and feeling abandoned. A singer doing the set might take the opportunity to act that transition from hopefulness to disappointment between songs two and three in a rather long silent pause, without losing character. As is the case in all the songs of this set, this woman's emotions are unusually hot. She loves more passionately and thoroughly than most people. In earlier times there were few economic opportunities for women. How will she survive on her own? I believe that in the fourth verse her reference to dyeing her dress red is a temporary thought that prostitution is her fate.

### When Johnny Comes Marchin' Home

She begins the song in an anxious daze, forcing herself to believe that Johnny will return. The anxiety builds through the fourth verse climax, then slows to her final series of repeated worry: "When?"

Richard Walters
May, 2007

**Richard Walters** (b. 1956) is a composer especially interested in writing for the voice. His numerous original compositions, including nine song cycles, remain largely unpublished. His unique style of concert arrangements for the recital stage makes art song treatments of folksongs, hymns, carols and popular standards. These have been published in several volumes, and have been recorded by various artists; they are widely performed. Walters has had a longtime career in music publishing, with editing credits for publications numbering in the hundreds, including the *G. Schirmer American Aria Anthology*, the *Oratorio Anthology* and over 60 other editions in *The Vocal Library* series, *The Singer's Musical Theatre Anthology*, and many other publications. He is Vice President of Classical Publications at Hal Leonard Corporation, a division of the company which includes G. Schirmer, Boosey & Hawkes, and North American representation of various European classical publishers. Richard was educated with a bachelor's degree in piano from Simpson College, where he studied coaching and accompanying with Robert Larsen, and composition with Sven Lekberg. His graduate study in composition was with Dominick Argento at the University of Minnesota. Walters has produced and performed on hundreds of recordings, and has had a versatile career as a musician. He is also a longtime classical music critic in Milwaukee.

### *Concert Arrangements for voice and piano by Richard Walters*
in The Vocal Library, published by Hal Leonard Corporation

**American Folksongs**
00740187 High Voice • 00740188 Low Voice

**The Christmas Collection**
00740153 High Voice • 00740154 Low Voice

**12 Christmas Favorites** (book/CD package)
00000384 High Voice • 00000385 Low Voice

**Classical Carols** (book/CD package)
00747024 High Voice • 00747025 Low Voice

**The Classical Singer's Christmas Album** (book/CD package)
00740062 High Voice • 00740063 Low Voice

**Folksongs in Recital** (book/CD package)
00000473 High Voice • 00000474 Low Voice

**Hymn Classics** (book/CD package)
00740033 High Voice • 00740032 Low Voice

**Popular Ballads for Classical Singers**
00740138 High Voice • 00740139 Low Voice

**The Sacred Collection**
00740155 High Voice • 00740156 Low Voice

**14 Sacred Solos** (book/CD package)
00740292 High Voice • 00740293 Low Voice

**Kathleen Sonnentag**, mezzo-soprano. "Rich," "Glorious," "Enveloping," are just a few adjectives that critics have used to describe Kathleen's mezzo-soprano voice. As the recipient of the prestigious Eleanor Steber Award for Excellence in the Concert Field, Ms. Sonnentag is known for the beauty and sincerity she brings to her music. She has been heard in Handel's *Messiah* in well over seventy-five performances from Chicago's Orchestra Hall to Tokyo's Hitomi Memorial Hall. A frequent soloist with the Milwaukee Symphony Orchestra, she has sung Bach's *Magnificat*, Beethoven's *Mass in C*, Bruckner's *Te Deum* and Bernstein's *Trouble in Tahiti*, among others. She has sung with the Japan Shinsei Symphony in Mendelssohn's *Paulus*, the Virginia Symphony in *Mozart's Requiem*, the Dayton Philharmonic in Beethoven's *Ninth Symphony*, and numerous orchestras throughout the Midwest. She has sung recitals in Illinois, Indiana, Iowa, Florida, South Dakota, Wisconsin and Chile. Excelling in opera as well, she has sung the leading roles in *Carmen, La Cenerentola, Hansel and Gretel,* and *The Marriage of Figaro*. *Opera News* praised her as "vocally commanding" for her role of Maddalena in *Rigoletto*. Ms. Sonnentag was selected by Marilyn Horne to sing in her first master class series at Carnegie Hall in New York. She was the First Place winner of the district Metropolitan Opera Auditions and a finalist in the *International Belvedere Competition* in Vienna. Ms. Sonnentag has recorded for Hal Leonard Corporation since 1991, and is featured on many book/CD releases, including *14 Sacred Solos, Sacred Classics, The Classical Singer's Christmas Album, Classical Carols, 12 Christmas Favorites, Wedding Classics*, and many others. Additional recordings of various songs and arias can be found at www.halleonard.com.

Distinguished American baritone **Kurt Ollmann** first came to prominence singing Riff on the Deutsche Grammophon recording of *West Side Story* under Leonard Bernstein. His operatic career has since taken him to La Scala, the Vienna State Opera, the Rome Opera, Brussels' La Monnaie and the Wexford Festival, as well as the Seattle, Washington, Los Angeles, Santa Fe, Glimmerglass, and New York City Opera companies. He has sung with the London Symphony Orchestra, L'Orchestre de Paris, Rome's Accademia de Santa Cecilia, the New York Philharmonic, the St. Paul Chamber Orchestra, and with the orchestras of Boston, Baltimore, Philadelphia and San Francisco, among many others. A noted recitalist, Mr. Ollmann studied the song literature with Gérard Souzay and Pierre Bernac and has made a specialty of the French and American classical song literature. He has appeared in recital at London's Wigmore Hall and in Paris, Milan, Geneva, New York, Chicago and numerous other European and American cities with such pianist colleagues as Mary Dibbern, Steven Blier and Donald St. Pierre. A champion of new American music, he has premiered works by such composers as Leonard Bernstein, Ned Rorem, Michael Torke, Richard Danielpour and Peter Lieberson and appears regularly with the New York Festival of Song. He was one of the original performers of the AIDS Quilt Songbook. Kurt Ollmann has recorded songs of Leguerney with Mary Dibbern for Harmonia Mundi France, Roussel with Dalton Baldwin for EMI, Schumann with Michael Barrett for Koch, and song works of Rorem with the New York Festival of Song for New World Records and with the composer for Newport Classics. Among his many other recordings are Gounod's *Roméo et Juliette* with Placido Domingo on BMG, Gershwin's *Oh, Kay!* with Dawn Upshaw on Nonesuch, Bernstein's *Candide* and *West Side Story* on DG, Ravel's *L'Heure Espagnole* under Previn, and *Pelléas et Mélisande* on Opera d'Oro. He has also been featured in several PBS specials. Mr. Ollmann has recorded for Hal Leonard Corporation since 2004. He is on the voice faculty at the University of Wisconsin-Milwaukee.

# Beware, Oh, Take Care

19th Century American Folksong
arranged by Richard Walters

ware, young la - dies, they're fool - in' you. Be - ware, oh, take care.

3. They smoke, they chew, they wear fine shoes. Be -

ware, oh, take care. And in their pock - et is a bot - tle o' booze. Be -

4. They

hold their hands up to their heart. They sigh, oh, they sigh. _____ They

say they love no one but you. _____ They lie, oh, they

lie. Be - ware, young la - dies, they're fool - in' you. Trust them not, they're

*8vb*

# Sail Around

19th Century American Folksong of the Plains
arranged by Richard Walters

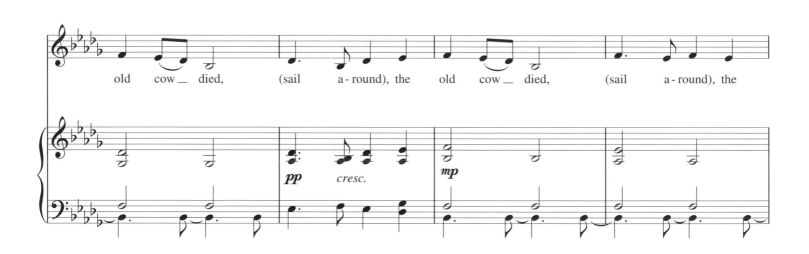

what the world ailed her? Did she die of the chol-er-a? Yes,\_\_\_\_ ma'am\_\_\_\_

The old cow\_ died, (sail a-round), the old cow\_ died,

(sail a-round).\_\_\_\_ Did the buz-zards, they come?\_ Yes, ma'am. Did the

buz-zards, they eat her? Yes, ma'am And did

# How Can I Keep from Singing

American Folksong
arranged by Richard Walters

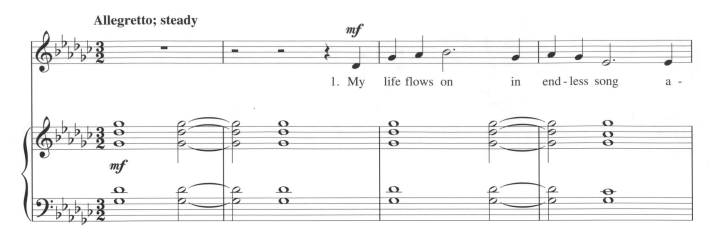

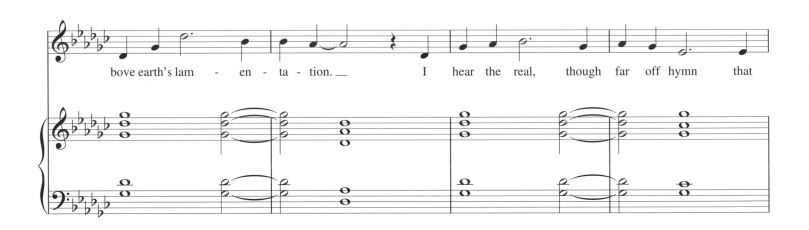

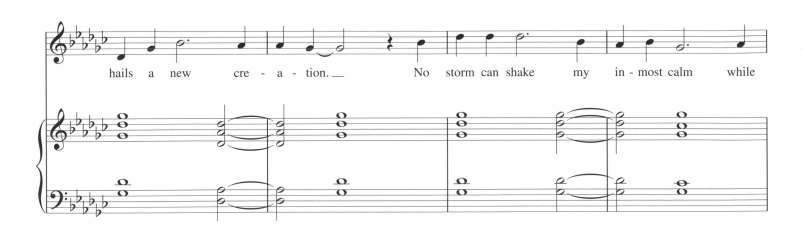

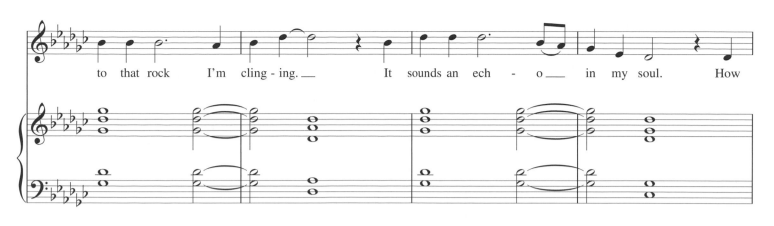

to that rock I'm cling-ing. __ It sounds an ech - o __ in my soul. How

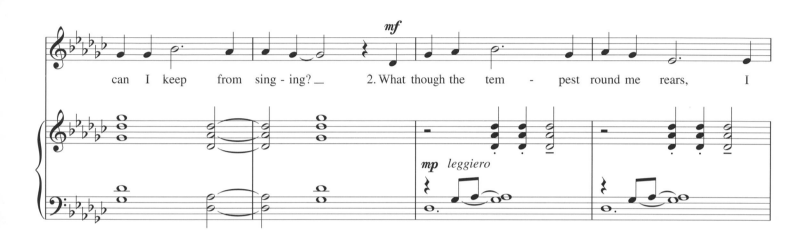

can I keep from sing-ing? __ 2. What though the tem - pest round me rears, I

know the truth, it liv-eth. __ What though the dark - ness round me close, Songs

in the night it giv-eth. __ No storm can shake my in-most calm while

to that rock I'm cling-ing. __ Since love is lord of __ Heav'n and earth How

can I keep from sing-ing? __

3. When ty-rants trem - ble, sick with fear And hear their death knells

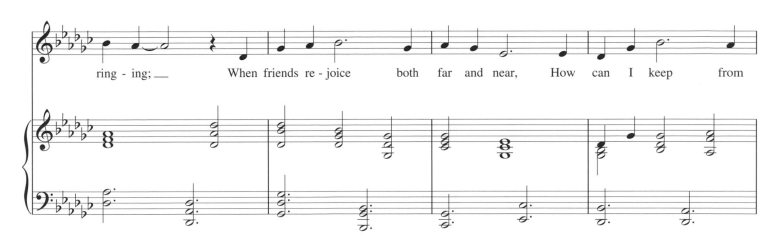

ring - ing; ___ When friends re - joice both far and near, How can I keep from

sing - ing? ___ In pris - on cell and dun-geon vile Our thoughts to them are

wing - ing. ___ When friends by shame are ___ un - de - filed, How can I keep from

# Once I Had a Sweetheart

Southern Appalachian Folksong
arranged by Richard Walters

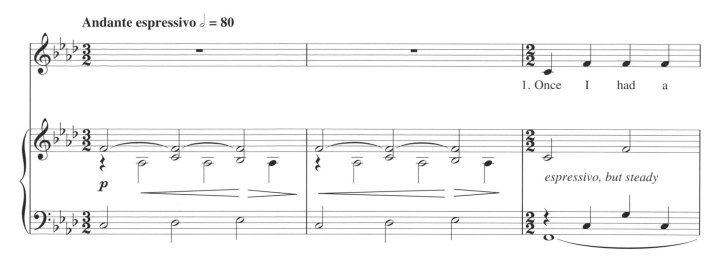

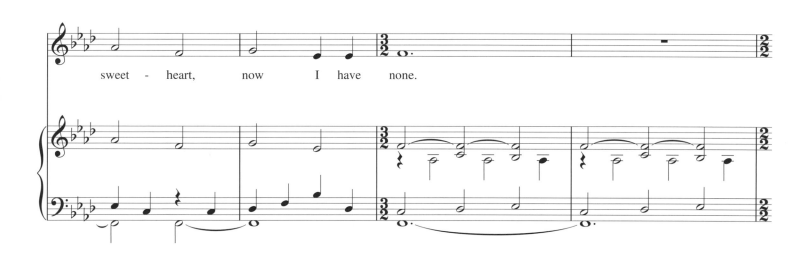

gone and left ___ me, he's gone and left ___ me. He's

gone and leaves ___ me to sor - row and

moan. ___ 2. He was such a

sweet - heart, oh, hap - py hours! ___

**Poco meno mosso** *dolce*

Once I had a sweet - heart, what have I now?

Twen - ty doz - en mem - 'ries, one bro - ken vow. _____

**Tempo primo**

He's gone and left __ me, he's gone __ and left __ me. He's gone __ and leaves __ me to

# Nine Hundred Miles

American Blues Folksong
arranged by Richard Walters

* pronounced "tuh" ("u" as in "put")

home to-mor-row night, __ 'cause I'm nine hun - dred miles from __ my

home. _____ And I hate t' hear that lone - some whis - tle

blow, _____ that long, lone - some train __ whis - tle

blow. _____ 2. Well, this

hate t' hear that lone-some whis-tle blow, _____ that

long, lone-some train ___ whis-tle blow. 3. Well, I'll

*mp*
*secco*

pawn you my watch, ___ and I'll pawn you my chain, ___ I'll

pawn you my gold-en dia-mond ring. And if this

*sim.*

train runs me right, __ I'll be home to - mor - row night, __ 'cause I'm

nine hun - dred, nine hun - dred, nine hun - dred miles from __ my

**Faster**

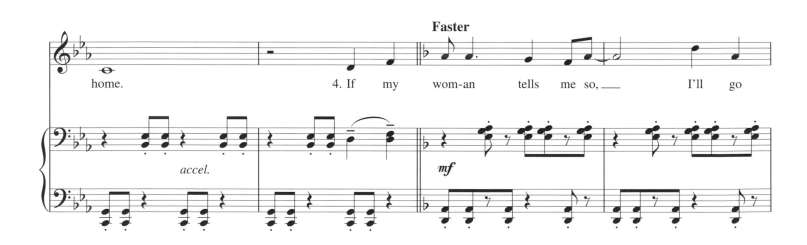

home. 4. If my wom - an tells me so, __ I'll go

*accel.*      *mf*

rail - road - in' no more, __ I'll side - track that wheel - er and go

*sim.*

hun - dred miles from my home.

(sub. **p**)

And I hate t'

hear that lone - some whis - tle blow,

that long,

sim.

# I Gave My Love a Cherry
## (The Riddle Song)

Folksong from the Kentucky Mountains
arranged by Richard Walters

end. I gave my love a ba-by with no cry - in'.

2. How can there be a cher - ry that has no stone? How can there be a chick-en that has no bone? How can there be a sto - ry that has no

end? How can there be a ba-by with no cry - in'?

(pp)

3. A cher - ry when it's

(p)

bloom-in', it has no stone. A chick-en when it's pip-pin', it

has no bone. The sto - ry that I love____ you,____ it

cresc. espr.

poco cresc. più esp.

has no _____ end. _____

A ba - by when it's sleep - in' makes no ____

cry - in'. _____

# Bill Groggin's Goat

Southern Appalachian Folksong
arranged by Richard Walters

**Lively** ♩ = 100

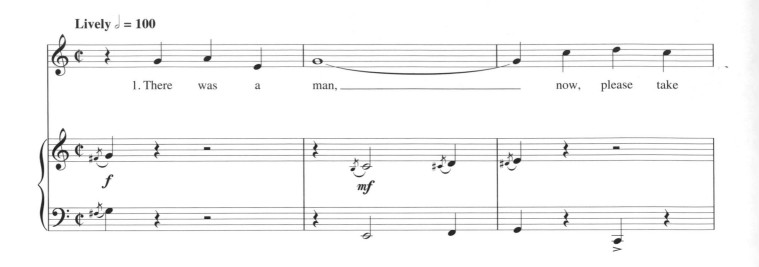

1. There was a man, _____ now, please take

note, there was a man _____

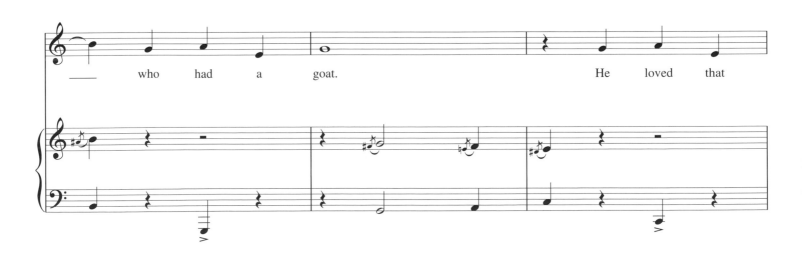

_____ who had a goat. He loved that

shirts _____ right off the line. The man, he

grabbed _____ him by the back _____ and tied him

to _____ a rail - road track.

3. Now, when the train _____ came in - to

sight, _____ that goat grew pale _____ and green with

fright. He heaved a sigh _____ as if in

pain, coughed up those shirts _____

and flagged the train. _____

# Shenandoah

19th Century American Chanty
arranged by Richard Walters

1. Oh, Shen-an-do', I long to hear you a-

way your roll-in' riv-er. Oh, Shen-an-do', I long to

hear you. A-way, I'm bound a-way 'cross the

* Missouruh

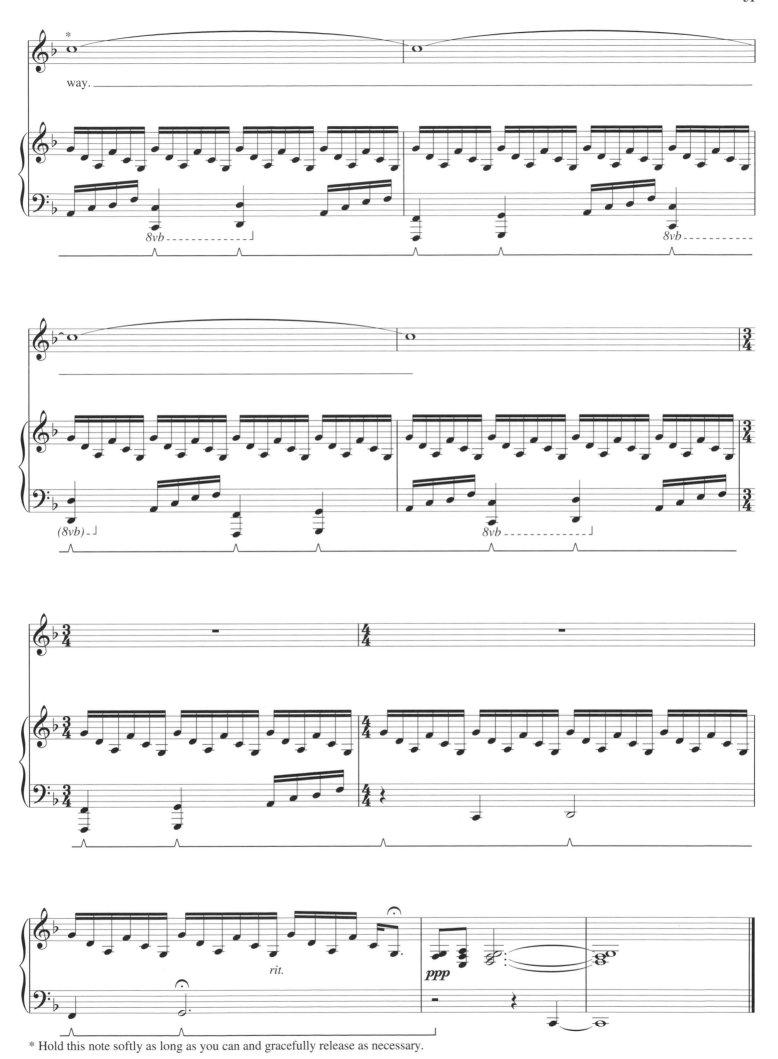

\* Hold this note softly as long as you can and gracefully release as necessary.

# Single Girl

19th Century American Folksong
arranged by Richard Walters

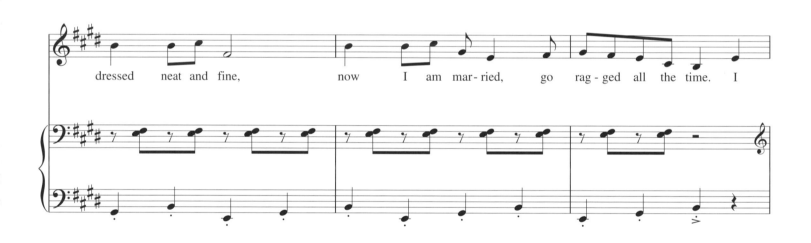

dressed neat and fine, now I am mar-ried, go rag-ged all the time. I

wish I were a sing-le girl a-gain, Lord, Lord, oh, I wish I were a sing-le girl a-gain.

54

* pronounced "tuh" ("u" as in "put")

gain.

*sub.* **f**    *sub.* ***p***    *sub.* **f**    *sub.* ***p***

**Slowly, freely** ♩ = 63

6. Wash them and dress them and put them to bed, be-

*rit.*    *sub.* **f**    *sub.* ***p***    *mp*

fore that drunk man curs - es us     and wish - es we were dead.     I

**Andante** ♩ = 80     ***p*** , *rit.*

*opt.*

wish I were a sing - le girl a - gain, Lord, Lord, oh I wish I were a sing - le girl a - gain.

***p***     *rit.*

# The Streets of Laredo

19th Century American Cowboy Song
based on the Irish Ballad "A Handful of Laurel"
arranged by Richard Walters

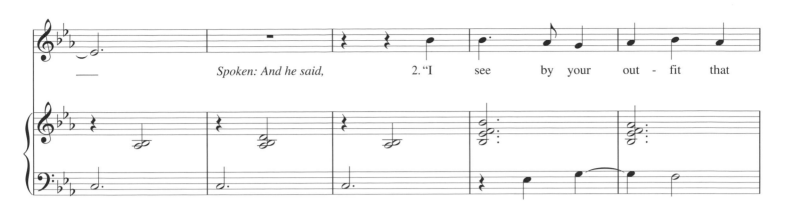

Spoken: And he said, 2. "I see by your out - fit that

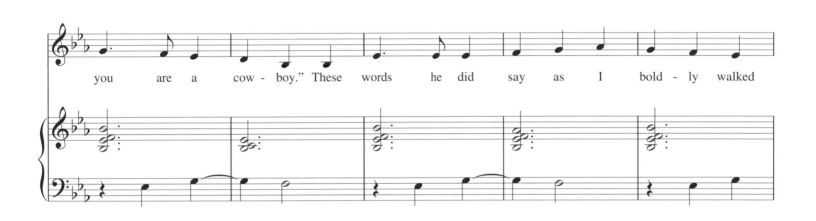

you are a cow - boy." These words he did say as I bold - ly walked

by. _____ "Come sit down be - side me and

hear my sad sto - ry. I'm shot in the chest and I know I must

die. _____

3. It was once in the sad-dle I

*warmly R.H. cantabile*

*p*  *mp*  *decresc.*

used    to go dash-in', once in the sad-dle I used to ride a-

way. _____ first down there to Ro - sie's and

then to the card-house. Got shot in the chest and I'm dy-in' to-

day.

4. Get six-teen gam-blers to car-ry my cof-fin. Get

six jol-ly cow-boys to sing me a song.

Take me to the grave - yard and lay the sod o'er me, for

I'm a young cow - boy and I know I've done wrong.

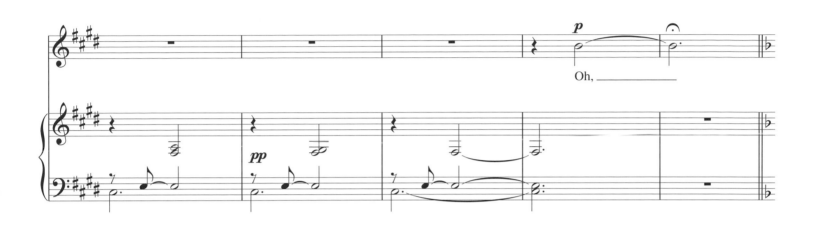

**Slowly** ♩ = 63
*(throughout this verse he becomes increasingly "sleepy" with death)*

bang    the    drum    slow - ly _____    and

play    the    fife    low - ly, _____

play the dead march as you car - ry me a - long. _____

Lay bunch - es of ros - es _____

all o - ver my cof - fin, ___ ros - es to

dead - en the clods as they fall. _____

*Johnny Songs*

# 1. I Know Where I'm Goin'

Scottish Folksong
arranged by Richard Walters

64

*Johnny Songs*
# 2. The Cruel War Is Raging

American Folksong from the Civil War
arranged by Richard Walters

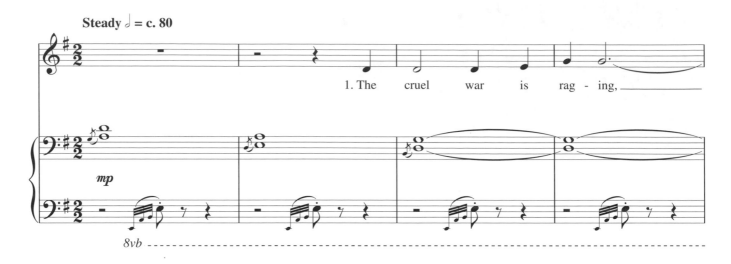

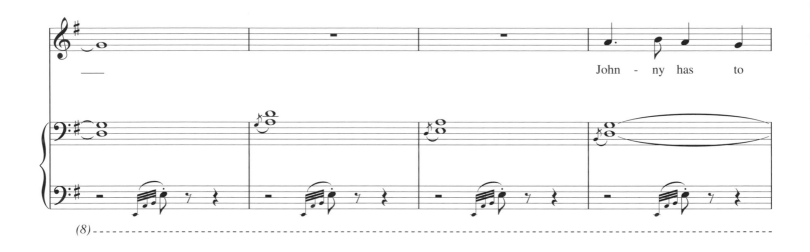

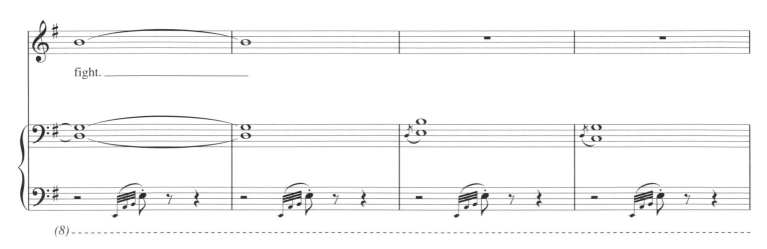

Sun - day, Mon - day is the day your cap - tain will call you and you must o - bey. _____ Your cap - tain will __ call you, it grieves __ my heart so. Won't you __ let me go with you? "No, my love, no." _____

"No, my love." No!

**Andante espressivo** ♩ = 88

5. John - ny, oh, John - ny, I fear you are un -

kind, for ____ I love _____ you far bet - ter than

all of man - kind. I _____

love _____ you far bet - ter than words can e'er ex - press. Won't you

let me go with you?

*(hesitantly)*
"Yes, my love, yes," _____

**Broadly**

**Tempo I**

*sub.* **pp**

*p*

*(non. rit.)*
**pp**

* another option

love _____ you far

*Johnny Songs*
# 3. Johnny Has Gone for a Soldier

American Revolutionary War Song
arranged by Richard Walters

1. There I sat on But-ter-milk Hill.

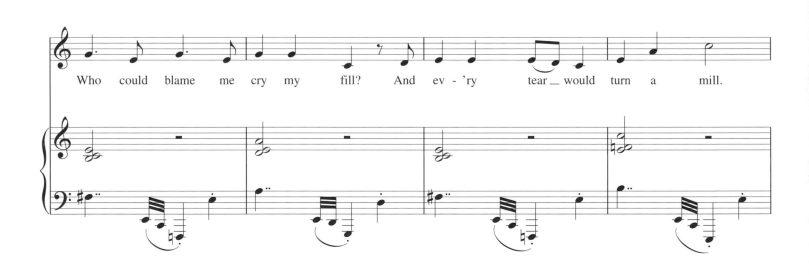

Who could blame me cry my fill? And ev-'ry tear __ would turn a mill.

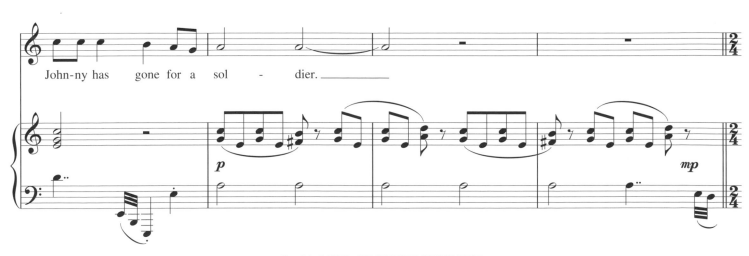

John-ny has gone for a sol - dier. _____

*espressive but steady*

2. Me oh my, I loved him so; broke my heart to see him go, and on - ly time __ will heal my woe. John-ny has gone for a sol - dier. _____

3. I'll sell my rod, I'll

sell my reel, like - wise I'll sell my spin - nin' wheel and

buy my love __ a sword of steel. John - ny has gone for a

sol - dier. _____

**Largo**
(***p***)

4. I'll dye my dress, I'll __ dye it red

*mf*

*mp*  *slow roll*

*mf*

*Johnny Songs*

# 4. When Johnny Comes Marchin' Home

American
Credited to Louis Lambert, 1863
Melody adapted from an Irish Folksong
arranged by Richard Walters

shout hur - ray when John-ny comes march - in' home.

3. The old church bell will peal with joy hur -

rah; _____ hur - rah to wel - come home our dar - lin' boy hur -

# About the Enhanced CD

In addition to piano accompaniments playable on both your CD player and computer, this enhanced CD also includes tempo adjustment and transposition software for computer use only. This software, known as Amazing Slow Downer, was originally created for use in pop music to allow singers and players the freedom to independently adjust both tempo and pitch elements. Because we believe there may be valuable educational use for these features in classical and theatre music, we have included this software as a tool for both the teacher and student. For quick and easy installation instructions of this software, please see below.

In recording a piano accompaniment we necessarily must choose one tempo. Our choice of tempo, phrasing, *ritardandos*, and dynamics is carefully considered. But by the nature of recording, it is only one option.

However, we encourage you to explore your own interpretive ideas, which may differ from our recordings. This new software feature allows you to adjust the tempo up and down without affecting the pitch. Likewise, Amazing Slow Downer allows you to shift pitch up and down without affecting the tempo. We recommend that these new tempo and pitch adjustment features be used with care and insight. Ideally, you will be using these recorded accompaniments and Amazing Slow Downer for practice only.

The audio quality may be somewhat compromised when played through the Amazing Slow Downer. This compromise in quality will not be a factor in playing the CD audio track on a normal CD player or through another audio computer program.

## INSTALLATION INSTRUCTIONS:

### For Macintosh OS 8, 9 and X:
- Load the CD-ROM into your CD-ROM Drive on your computer.
- Each computer is set up a little differently. Your computer may automatically open the audio CD portion of this enhanced CD and begin to play it.
- To access the CD-ROM features, double-click on the data portion of the CD-ROM (which will have the Hal Leonard icon in red and be named as the book).
- Double-click on the "Amazing OS 8 (9 or X)" folder.
- Double-click "Amazing Slow Downer"/"Amazing X PA" to run the software from the CD-ROM, or copy this file to your hard disk and run it from there.
- Follow the instructions on-screen to get started. The Amazing Slow Downer should display tempo, pitch and mix bars. Click to select your track and adjust pitch or tempo by sliding the appropriate bar to the left or to the right.

### For Windows:
- Load the CD-ROM into your CD-ROM Drive on your computer.
- Each computer is set up a little differently. Your computer may automatically open the audio CD portion of this enhanced CD and begin to play it.
- To access the CD-ROM features, click on My Computer then right click on the Drive that you placed the CD in. Click Open. You should then see a folder named "Amazing Slow Downer". Click to open the "Amazing Slow Downer" folder.
- Double-click "setup.exe" to install the software from the CD-ROM to your hard disk. Follow the on-screen instructions to complete installation.
- Go to "Start," "Programs" and find the "Amazing Slow Downer" folder. Go to that folder and select the "Amazing Slow Downer" software.
- Follow the instructions on-screen to get started. The Amazing Slow Downer should display tempo, pitch and mix bars. Click to select your track and adjust pitch or tempo by sliding the appropriate bar to the left or to the right.
- Note: On Windows NT, 2000 and XP, the user should be logged in as the "Administrator" to guarantee access to the CD-ROM drive. Please see the help file for further information.

## MINIMUM SYSTEM REQUIREMENTS:

### For Macintosh:
Power Macintosh; Mac OS 8.5 or higher; 4 MB Application RAM; 8x Multi-Session CD-ROM drive

### For Windows:
Pentium, Celeron or equivalent processor; Windows 95, 98, ME, NT, 2000, XP; 4 MB Application RAM; 8x Multi-Session CD-ROM drive